First Printing, 2012

ISBN 978-1-105-42966-8

Jennifer Smith
Champaign, IL

http://www.lulu.com/content/paperback-book/
learning-to-live-legendary/12414019

Contents

To my favorite; I love you most!

Foreword

In *Learning to Live Legendary*, Jennifer Smith shares the Magic 7 with her readers. Like huge, dazzling displays of fireworks going off in the night sky, these 7 memories explode with joy and wonderment—proving that goodness can illuminate the dark. But just as remarkable as those spectacular explosions of color and light are, so too are the still, mysterious periods of Jennifer's life, which reveal the quiet complexity of her unique journey and nature.

In one of her darker moments, Jennifer was diagnosed with breast cancer. She was 30 years-old at the time, and she learned that battling this disease at such a young age is particularly challenging. To begin, there are issues of fertility. For postmenopausal women who are diagnosed, they likely have made their families; they do not have to think about having their fertility compromised. In addition, young women with breast cancer are oftentimes still working and building a career, and cancer can derail those plans. Then there are the physical changes that accompany cancer treatment, and their affect upon one's body image and sexuality. And yes: there is the responsibility of caring for an existing family. How does, for instance, a mother in treatment care for her children? How does she have the strength? How can she take care of others when she can barely brush her own teeth or make it up the stairs? And, in reality, sometimes partners don't stick around; and as sad as this is, it is a reality—a hardship. This is why, Jen states, we must be ever-mindful of our young survivors and be a light unto them—for they are in great need.

But from these dark moments have come enlightening realizations. She has learned, for example, to live *in* the moment. Whether that means going for a bike ride with her son or having dinner with her family, she has learned not to be distracted by an ever-growing "to-do" list. She has learned to automatically prioritize what is important to her. For her, there is a sense of urgency to life. Time can't be wasted, and she wants to spend it with people closest to her. Understandably, Jennifer wishes that she didn't have to learn such lessons the hard way, and she hopes others can learn it more easily. We can learn, for instance, to stop obsessing about the future and just be still—in the moment. We can let go of the notion of the "the next best thing" and embrace the present.

When asked how she deals with the present moment when it is dark and miserable, she said that we will all have those moments, and that for her, faith and hope give her strength. One year after the date of her initial lumpectomy, Jennifer had a cross with a pink ribbon hanging from it tattooed on her left foot. For her, the tattoo is a reminder that faith and hope will sustain her. She also reminds herself that we are all suffering. She is not different.

In *Learning to Live Legendary*, Jennifer relishes the remarkable periods of light and love, and perhaps it is because she is not afraid to die that she embraces the beauty of the moment. It's not that she wants to die, she says, but she thinks of death as a "Welcome Home" party, of sorts. She will be going somewhere even more incredible—somewhere that will reunite her with her grandparents, her cousins, and even the little baby she miscarried when she was undergoing fertility treatments before Corbin. For Jennifer, her life doesn't end at death, and she will be waiting for all of her friends and family—and especially dear Corbin—to join her one day.

Oh, yes: there is Corbin. She adores so much about her son. There is his laugh and his sense of humor, and Jennifer says that he just loves to be funny—he loves telling jokes. She particularly relishes in his belly laugh—the kind of laugh that surfaces on exciting rollercoaster rides and during bouts of unrestrained tickling. There is much that Jennifer wants to teach her son, but she realizes there is much that Corbin has also taught her. He has reminded her to not take life so seriously. Sometimes, for example, when Corbin wants to play and make a mess, she will initially hesitate; then, though, she reminds herself to live in the moment, and she goes for it. Still, she is ever the mother. She would like to always be present to teach and protect her son. She wants to teach him, first and foremost, to be compassionate. She wants so much for him—as any parent does for her child, and she wants him to be fulfilled, to be giving, and to find someone one day who fulfills him—who is his best friend and his favorite person to be around. She wants him to know who his true friends are and to show empathy toward those who are not. She hopes he will value learning and be ever-curious. But in those dark moments, she would want Corbin to remember that she is forever with him and that she is *always* his loving, devoted mother, and that no mother could love her son more than she does him.

If Jennifer could ask for one wish, she would ask that we each embrace all the present moments of our lives: the big, brilliant exploding moments in the night sky as well as the still, private moments in between. She would ask that we that we search for quality not quantity—that we love deeply and authentically—that we let go and laugh our deep belly laughs.

Teri Fuller
Young Breast Cancer Survivor and Advocate

When I was first diagnosed, I received hundreds of cards. For years, I kept them in a box. I didn't want to throw away peoples' good wishes, kind words, and thoughtful prayers, but I didn't know what to do with the cards. One year from the day of my surgery, I got a tattoo of a cross with a pink ribbon hanging on it on my left foot. To me, it symbolized that I couldn't have gotten through my breast cancer journey without my faith. The cover image is an interpretation of my tattoo. It is a collage made from the cards people sent. I incorporated words that empowered me during this journey: believe, faith in God, laugh loud, hope, patience, courage and more. The cross is made out of these words; it is also made out of my family's signatures because they are my true pillar.

Preface

**As I grow to understand life less and less,
I learn to love it more and more.**
Jules Renard

For many years, people have told me "write a book." At last,
on October 11, 2011, I sat down at my computer to do just
that: to write. I began by turning on iTunes and shuffled my
"chill" songs for accompaniment while writing. The first
song that randomly played was "If I Die Young" by The
Band Perry. The lead singer, Kimberly Perry, of the sibling
trio sings: "A penny for my thoughts? Oh no, I'll sell em for
a dollar; they're worth so much more after I'm a goner." My
hope, however, is that these thoughts will be read before I'm
a goner. In the past four years, I've spent a lot of time
thinking about dying, death, and what it all means. I have lost
numerous close friends, planned my funeral, written my
obituary, and paid for my spot in the columbarium at my
church. But, this book isn't about sadness, sorrow, or death.
It's quite the opposite, actually. After being diagnosed with a
terminal form of breast cancer at thirty-one, I have spent
much of my time learning how to live and enjoy every
precious moment of my life. I have realized my time is truly a
priceless commodity and to be shared only with those adding
to my quality of life. I have discovered how to *Live Legendary*
and I have spent far more time *Living Legendary* and cheating
death than thinking about dying.

I didn't always know how to *Live Legendary*. I grew up middle class, and ran with a core group of friends in high school. I didn't win any awards for sports or academics. I wasn't the prom queen or voted "best in class" for anything. I continued on in my life with a to-do list of things: college, career, marriage, family, etc… but that list never had anything *legendary*. I can't attribute just one moment to the change. I was thirty years young when I found the lump in my right breast. I remember telling a few friends; they dismissed it by telling me it was a clogged milk duct. They had a point; I was nursing my eight-month old son when I found it. I am 5'11", ate healthy, and in good shape. I worked out regularly. I didn't even have cavities. I volunteered. I felt like I was a good person! When I found the lump, I also assumed it was a clogged milk duct from breast feeding. I had a clogged duct before, but this felt different. My clogged duct, confirmed by the breast feeding clinic, was painful. I used heat and gentle massage and the painful lump disappeared. This lump didn't hurt. It felt like a dime sized rock under the skin, and it wasn't going away. At my son's nine-month baby check-up, I looked at his pediatrician and said, "I know you treat children, but I found a lump." She was the one who encouraged me to get it checked out. I later learned she had another young mom in her practice recently diagnosed with breast cancer.

I also can't attribute *Learning to Live Legendary* to when the cancer came back in 2008 when I was thirty-one. It is usually considered a fast recurrence when breast cancer comes back within a year of completing treatment. I had my first scan three months after completing treatment. I remember walking down the hall with the radiologist to view the results when I saw my radiation oncologist and head chemo nurse through the window. I started to crumble and burst in to tears. I knew. Screaming, "NO!!! NO!!! NO!!!" I started to collapse; my mom and husband held me up. Realizing this very emotional scene was in the middle of a public hallway, I said, "Get me out of the hall." Sheer panic raged through my body knowing horrific news was coming. When we entered the radiologist's dimly lit office surrounded by computer monitors with images of my scans, I simply said, "Where the fuck is it?" The radiologist calmly explained there were several areas, or hot spots, in my bones where cancerous lesions were growing. I'd already endured a lumpectomy, six grueling months of biweekly chemotherapy, and seven weeks of daily radiation—a colossal amount of treatment, and somehow it had spread to my bones. Now that the cancer spread outside of the breast, it was a diagnosis of Stage IV, meaning it is considered incurable and terminal. I was thirty-one and forced to confront the illusion of immortality.

And maybe most amazingly, I can't attribute *Learning to Live Legendary* to filing and going through a divorce while being in treatment for Stage IV breast cancer. I was not in a supportive and satisfying marriage, but I was utterly devastated when I learned my husband had led a double life our entire marriage. I still don't know the whole story, and I'm okay with that. What I do know is that it has more twists and drama than a Lifetime movie. I know that I loved the illusion of a person. I also know what a relief it is to not have to worry about stories that don't add up, lies, and broken promises.

So many times, I've heard, "Keep up the fight." I wonder, though: what am I really fighting? My body? Cancer wasn't the first time I've had my body fail me. We unsuccessfully tried to conceive for a year before I underwent multiple rounds of infertility treatments. I want to love my body, yet it's the enemy, and I'm trapped inside. Society is hard enough on women, so seeing as I'm 5'11", slender, and have high cheekbones, you might think I love my body. I do: now. After rounds of infertility treatment, a miscarriage, cancer, countless surgeries leaving scars everywhere, millions of dollars in treatment leaving me bald twice (so far), I do finally love my body. Because inside my body is what really matters. The body is just a vessel–full of imperfections. It succumbs to cancer. It isn't as strong and powerful as we'd like to believe. It's what the vessel holds that is sublime and beautiful and transcendent. It's ironic that as I became even more scarred and mutilated, my spirit and sense of self worth became stronger and more empowered. My grace, compassion, integrity, sense of humor, and desire to *Live Legendary* is contagious. Or at least I hope. I often joke, "I have cancer, not cooties; don't worry, I'm not contagious." But this piece of me…who I am at the core -*that*- is what I've learned from this journey. I hope to share a glimpse of it with you in recalling the "Magic 7 of 2011." This book is a tribute to all of you—you who made the Magic 7 happen. For you, I thank you.

Xoxo
Jen

The Magic 7 of 2011

Magic 1: Turning Ordinary into Extraordinary

I may never know the meaning of life, but once my son was born I felt my life had true meaning.
Darren Maddern

My love affair with scrapbooking started in high school. I enjoyed putting the photographs on the page to capture the memories. My parents kept simple photo albums, but I enjoyed enhancing the pages to tell a story as I captured the memory. The scrapbook page seemed to anchor the event in my mind. I created elaborate pages to capture the big moments in my life. At that time, before everything was digital, I enjoyed picking up my prints and seeing what magic had been captured on film. I would go home and spend hours designing pages in my scrapbooks. Now, I love looking at the scrapbooks I made—full of memories from our high-school youth group go-and-serve. We participated in the Appalachian Service Project, traveling to remote parts of the Appalachia mountain range to work repairing homes of those in severe poverty. Those trips were the start of shaping my core love of helping others. I also now look back and remember the adventure of spring break trips in college. Crammed in a van with close friends, we drove over twenty-four hours to our sunny destinations for a week of carefree fun. My scrapbooks document relationships, friendships, and significant milestones in my life including my wedding and the birth of my son, Corbin.

It's funny because once I became pregnant, I no longer wanted to scrapbook. Some people develop food aversions while pregnant. I, on the other hand, developed a scrapbooking aversion. I had no desire to create scrapbooks anymore, but I still love taking pictures. But, I'm realistic: I know I'm a complete amateur. It takes someone with true artistic talent and an incredible eye to capture priceless memories. I continually try and I consider it a "happy accident" if I'm able to capture a glimpse of a special moment.

Just after I had Corbin, I saw a beautiful picture of a coworker's child so I contacted the photographer, Allyson Sanborn of Sweet Pea Photography. Allyson took Corbin's six month, one year, and eighteen month pictures. However, after I learned that my cancer had returned and spread to my bones, I was so absorbed in *cancerland* that I forgot to schedule Corbin's two year pictures. Then add the divorce and ensuing economic hardship to the cancerland landscape, and I fell way off the photograph wagon.

So the last time I worked with Allyson was spring 2008. In the time since then, Allyson has contacted me several times offering her services. I didn't want to use my health problems as a way to take advantage of her, so I politely declined. Still, she persisted. She then told me she wanted to capture an "ordinary day" with Corbin and me. It was January of 2011, and I was bald once more when I welcomed her into my home. Corbin was wearing jeans and a comfy blue sweatshirt with a police badge on the chest. I was wearing jeans, a cozy charcoal gray turtle neck and signature scarf on my bald head. Allyson introduced herself before she blended into the background and snapped away. We played with Corbin's train set, read books such as *How Big is a Million?*, and looked through the latest memory book I made him. We played Candy Land, colored, and most importantly: we laughed.

Less than a week later, she sent me an email with a link to the slideshow. She also gave me the CD of images and copyright release. The photographs were beyond breathtaking! They truly captured an ordinary day in an absolutely extraordinary way! They show the astonishing bond between a mother and child. They captured emotions of happiness, tenderness, and most importantly: love. The pictures remind me that these ordinary moments are just as incredible, if not more so, than the big moments. Often we overlook *ordinary* in search of extraordinary memories. Being a mother has given my life true meaning, and I'm so thankful that Allyson helped me to capture an *ordinary* day.

The pictures are incredibly intimate and provide a glimpse into my safe haven: my home. After my divorce, when I purchased my home, I decided the only people allowed in it were people whom I knew and trusted. Allyson was definitely someone I trusted. However, sharing the pictures on my blog was something I struggled with. I knew that so many would see the amazing love and bond that Corbin and I share. But that would mean that they would be gaining access to my private oasis.

Nonetheless, I decided to share them. The amazing support of so many people on my blog looking at the pictures crashed the website. There were pictures of me with hats, scarves, and some with just my bald head. But the funny thing is: the pictures weren't about my diagnosis; they were about an extraordinary bond between a mother and son. Someone commented: "The images are so evocative of love and life, not illness." Once I read that comment I had peace and confidence that sharing the brilliant talent of Allyson was the right decision. The photographs captured who my son and I are—not what has happened to us. In some ways, I am relieved. I am relieved that no matter what happens; my son and I know love and life. The hard part then was finding enough wall space to display all the stunning photographs. Here are a few of my personal favorites.

7

Magic 2: The Travel Bug

Happiness is not a station you arrive at,
but a manner of traveling.
Margaret Lee Runbeck

In the summer of 2010, I was visiting my dad's extended family in Cleveland, Ohio. I went to dinner with Mollie, one of my college girlfriends, a few of her friends from Cleveland, my sister, and my Stage IV friend, Erin, who was also in town visiting her family. Erin and her husband live in Orlando, Florida so it was delightful to see her while we were both traveling to see family. While at dinner, one of the girls asked Erin what she did for a living. She boldly said, "My job is to be healthy. I get massages, go to yoga, juice, stay up to date on research, and stay away from stress." Erin not only taught me that being a Stage IV cancer patient is a full time job, but she also taught me that even though we're dealing with a life threatening illness, we still have much we can do. One of the things that she was most passionate about was traveling, and she encouraged me to do so as well.

In February 2011, I went to Orlando for a young women's breast cancer conference. Including Erin, there were five of us "roommates" who attended the conference together. All five of us were young (forty and under) and living with Stage IV breast cancer. These incredible ladies *get it* in a way no one else possibly could. The median age of diagnosis is sixty-one, so being diagnosed so young (thirty years young for me) often feels isolating. This conference focuses exclusively on young women with breast cancer and what cutting edge research is revealing. It also offers opportunities to meet others in a similar situation–others who *get it*. We can't help but form a powerful community—a community that reminds us that we are not alone.

One evening the five of us were sitting around the pool discussing how our paths have crossed. We never expected to meet each other, and now we were able to understand and love each other in a way that few can relate. We laughed about embarrassing moments due to wig malfunctions, discussed our fears, and talked about the legacies we hoped to leave behind.

While sitting there, we were approached by one of the vendors who was making a video for ABC's "Your Three Words." I agreed to participate and my three words were I LOVE LIVING. While they filmed me, my four roommates decided on their three words as a group: BELIEVE IN MIRACLES. Just then, the battery in the video camera died. The vendor retreated to the hotel in hopes of charging the battery. We wanted to capture the moment so we took a picture with a camera and continued on in conversation and didn't think much of it. A few weeks after the conference, my phone was blowing up with messages from friends who saw me on a lead-in to a story about cancer on the ABC nightly news. Apparently the video from the conference in Orlando made it to New York City. And for a split second, my three words made the national news.

Shayne, Erin, Marcia, Tracy, me –
Five Young Stage IV Ladies Loving Life

ABC's "Three Words"

After the conference in Orlando, my parents, sister, and Corbin flew down, and we went to the four Disney World theme parks. I had severe burns on the back of my left thigh and knee from radiation, but with ample topical pain medication we were able to get around and have a wonderful time. I can't decide on a favorite memory: getting to see my parents enjoy the magic of Disney with my son or hearing Corbin's uncontrollable belly laugh as we rode the runaway mine car rollercoaster (just don't tell my doctor I was on it!).

A Quiet Moment Before the Magic Begins

Sara, me, My Dad, My Mom
and, of course, Corbin at Epcot

After Orlando, I went on the ultimate girl's trip to the Big Island, Hawaii with my sister, Sara, and best friend, Ashley. My dad's cousin (whom I met once when I was twelve) has a house there and encouraged our visit. She sent the keys to the house and told us to have a wonderful time, which we did! Just a few months prior, before the trip was even planned, two very generous families gave me an unexpected financial gift. Once we booked our trip, I decided this money would be our "memory money" and pay for all of our adventures while on vacation.

We explored all of the Big Island. Forget bar hopping—we beach hopped! We slathered up with sunscreen and then hit the beach. We went to three different beaches in one day; and eight different beaches overall. We even tried body boarding and learned to complete a "suit check" before standing to make sure everything was covered. We also went snorkeling in the open water, and a pod of dolphins swam four feet in front of us! Later that evening, we got back in the pitch-black water with flashlights. A twelve-foot manta ray swooped beneath us doing barrel rolls as it ate the planktons which were attracted to the lights. The edges of this magnificent creature came within inches of us. In addition, we went on a helicopter tour of the volcano on the Big Island and saw a tiny bit of lava. Driving home from the helicopter tour, we relied too much on GPS and ended up on a road to nowhere, which at 13,000 feet surprisingly was *NOT* the tallest mountain in Hawaii. Then there was the food. Fresh fruit from the farmer's market every day and dessert every evening. And we laughed so hard we cried, many, *many* times.

Exploring the Big Island with Sara and Ashley

Really Excited to be in Hawaii!

Then in April, I was off to NYC for the OMG Cancer Summit hosted by Stupid Cancer, which seeks to uplift young adults with any type of cancer. I'd never been to NYC, but the chance to meet young adults who *get it* and explore a new city sounded like a great idea! I was able to stay with a great friend, and the conference registration was free.

The conference discussed relationship issues after being diagnosed, parenting after diagnosis, legal issues, being your own advocate, and more! The conference gave ample time for networking opportunities to talk with others who weren't afraid of the elephant in the room. They also created a powerful video documentary where young adults could look in the camera lens and tell cancer *exactly* what they thought.

After the conference was over, I walked and talked with one of the leaders in cancerland: Jonny Imerman. He founded Imerman Angels, which provides one-on-one support for someone newly diagnosed and matches them to a mentor angel who had the diagnosis. It's like Big Brothers Big Sisters in cancerland and one of my favorite cancer-related organizations! Jonny was familiar with the city, so we walked and saw many of the sights that weekend. We walked through Soho, Tribecca, had dessert at the famed Serendipity restaurant, went to the top of the Empire State building, and went on a carriage ride through Central Park.

In the Middle of Times Square, NYC

At the Top of the Empire State Building with
an Angel Himself – Jonny Imerman

April was over and it was on to May! Flashback to October 2008, I had just learned the cancer spread to my bones. I decided then that I wanted to take Corbin to Disney World before my health declined further preventing the trip. That trip ended up being over Mother's Day weekend in 2009. While we were at Disney World, I decided that each Mother's Day I would take Corbin to a different amusement park to make our own special tradition. In 2009, Disney World. In 2010 I took him to Six Flags in St. Louis. The next year when some of our good friends moved to Dallas, I naturally decided we would go visit them and go to Six Flags Over Texas for Mother's Day weekend in 2011. We had a "Texas sized Mother's Day" weekend! We rode rides, got soaked, laughed, and created amazing memories with some of our dearest friends.

Making Our Best "Roller Coaster Face"
at Six Flags Over Texas

Soaked With Memories

In the first five months of 2011, I traveled and explored more than I have in the past ten years. It was one step in *Learning to Live Legendary*. The experience of discovering new regions, cultures, and environments only made my addiction to travel intensify.

Magic 3: Dreams really DO come true!

The magic recipe to living out your boldest dreams:
A pinch of delusion, a dash of audacity,
and a shot of courage.
Kirsty Spraggon

When I was five, my family moved from Columbia, Missouri to Champaign, Illinois. While I vaguely remember Columbia, I associate my childhood with growing up in Champaign. Champaign is a "Big 10" town with much of the focus on the University of Illinois' sports and Greek life. The campus has an urban feel and the area loyally follows the football and basketball teams. The University of Illinois also has one the largest Inter Greek systems in the nation. When preparing for college, I didn't apply to the University of Illinois, couldn't wait to get out town, and swore I'd never return to Champaign.

I planned on going to Western Illinois University. A visit to their campus showed it was located even more in the cornfields of Illinois than Champaign. Jessi, my best friend in high school, asked me to go with her to an open house in Carbondale at Southern Illinois University. Whereas the University of Illinois was famed for its sports and Greek life, Southern was famed for its excessive partying and riotous Halloween festivities.

When we arrived to the SIU campus, it was such a stark contrast to the urban feel on the campus of the University of Illinois. There was a lake on campus and a wooded area I could walk through on my way to class. The Greek system was small, less than ten percent of the student body. I felt that I was at home and instantly decided this would be where I attend college.

I was an athletic training major, combining my two loves of sports and helping people. I was rooming with Jessi and remember trying to decide whether to rush that first semester. I chose to wait a semester to make sure I had the academics and demanding athletic training observation hours under control before joining the Greek system.

Compared to the castle-like sorority houses at the U of I, the sororities at SIU were old dormitories. I rushed the second semester of my freshman year. Many people question whether the Greek system is just "buying friends," but let me tell you: I made life-long friends while in my sorority, and these girls have been the ones by my side during my toughest times. They have also been with me during the best times and even sent me soaring on one of the highest parts of my life.

There were seven of us who ran around together:

Jessi—the entrepreneur   Jill—the fashionista
Lindsay—the "Martha Stewart"   Emily—the nurse
Robin—the cheerleader   Mollie—the athlete

After college, we dispersed to all parts of the country for jobs, graduate schools, and family. We stayed in touch through email, getting together for each other's weddings, baby showers, and an annual girl's trip. One year we went to Marco Island, Florida. The next year we traveled to Lake of the Ozarks, Missouri when four of us were pregnant (and due within three months of each other).

Time was flying, but we didn't lose touch. We continually kept in touch through visits, emails, and phone calls. We celebrated each other's job accomplishments, weddings, and the birth of new children. This group was the first I told about my diagnosis. I remember one reacting calmly, in shock; another in hysteria, bawling. I remember the subsequent phone calls, texts, and updates regarding my health. In addition to my immediate family, they were the ones I would immediately text with health related updates. They offered prayers, laughter, companionship, and undying loyalty.

When I was in the middle of treatment in 2008, Jessi kept encouraging—wait, that isn't a strong enough word. Jessi keep nagging me to do The Breast Cancer 3 Day sponsored by Susan G. Komen. This was a sixty mile walk and fundraiser for breast cancer. Jessi had several family members diagnosed and wanted to walk in honor of them. I had completed four of the six months of chemo and still had seven weeks of daily radiation to finish. Utter exhaustion at that point was an understatement. I looked at the website, hoping to find an excuse to give Jessi. Then I noticed, the last event was in San Diego. I decided if I'm walking sixty miles in three days, I'm sure as hell NOT doing it in Illinois.

Walking along the coastline and beaches of San Diego in November? I could handle that. I emailed the rest of the group to see if anyone was interested. This meant committing to each raising $2200, training for the walk, and taking vacation time to *walk*. To my surprise six replied that they were in (the last one was pregnant and unable to go). My mom and sister joined us, and each person on our team walked ALL sixty miles. Just the month before the walk, I learned the cancer returned and spread to my bones. But my crew kept me company during all sixty miles! During the walk we discovered that pretzels and cream cheese are an addicting snack and incredibly motivating! We adapted to sleeping in tents and showering in mobile trucks! We also searched any store along the route to find our beloved Diet Coke since we were going through withdrawal. A few in our group were escorted back to the camp site by the San Jose police officers volunteering at the event. Apparently stopping at a bar along the route for happy hour was not calculated into the day and they needed guidance getting back. And, just when you thought you had seen EVERY possible way to make a pun about boobs, there was always one more that made you laugh.

This sisterhood embraced and uplifted me during one of my difficult periods: my divorce. At that time, my roommate in the sorority, Jill, decided each year we'd get together in March to celebrate my birthday. The weekend was sacred, just our group. In past years, we celebrated our weekend in Chicago. In 2011, we stayed at the beach house of a family friend on Lake Michigan in New Buffalo, Michigan. We didn't care that it was snowy outside; we enjoyed catching up with each other. We took walks along Lake Michigan, went shopping at an outlet mall, dined out, and went to a casino where one of us actually won money! Most importantly, we traded updates and funny stories about our children.

In sharing, I mentioned Corbin had been asking about going on the Disney Dream cruise since he "read" the advertisement booklet while potty training two years ago. He referred to it as the "boat with Lighting and Red." His favorite movie is *Cars*, and in a toddler mind, going on a huge ship with characters from the movie seemed like paradise! I kept stalling when he'd ask about going because I didn't think the boat was finished. It is also incredibly expensive, and he doesn't understand what a budget of a single mom with Stage IV cancer looks like. Being on disability cuts my income in half, then medical expenses (COBRA, deductibles, and medications) take almost another half which leaves very little room in the budget for vacation.

The week after our girl's weekend, I received a birthday card that said, "Call Jill when you open this." I opened the envelope and the front was Mickey Mouse and inside there was a birthday greeting and a link. I called Jill, opened the link, and read:

It is extremely hard to sit and write a "brief summary description" of Jen Smith because she is SO many things to all of us. She is a daughter, a sister, a mother, and an amazing friend. She is an inspiration, a leader, a mentor, and a Stage IV breast cancer warrior. Our group of girlfriends has gone through all life's ups and downs during our years at SIU until now. Death of family members, marriage, babies, divorce, heart break, joy, tears and new beginnings. We could handle it all together. But getting the news that at the young age of thirty, our dear friend was diagnosed with breast cancer was something that has turned all of our lives upside-down. Cancer. Just the word alone sucks the air right out of the room. We have watched our fearless, take-no-prisoner, tall, gorgeous, go-get-em' all, grab life by the horns, successful, admirable-friend Jen halted by this terrible disease. She has lost all her hair twice, has to constantly live with needles, shots, ports, IV's, scans, radiation, burns, chemo, sickness, fatigue, nausea, devastating news of cancer spreading, and clocking in countless hours in doctor's offices. But through all of this she still remains the fearless, take no prisoner, gorgeous, go-get-em' all, take on life and LOVES LIVING her life, friend Jen. Her smile radiates and you can only look at her and believe she can do anything.

But even when the mind and heart are strong, the body can be weak and there are some things she just can't do. But we can.

Living with Stage IV cancer for her is about QUALITY of LIFE, and our goal is to give her that quality and make her DREAMS come true. After all, when you wish upon a star, makes no difference who you are, anything your heart desires will come to you.

And I think we could all be that star she can wish on.

What better way to make her Dreams come true but to send Jen and her four-year old Disney's Lighting McQueen obsessed son, Corbin, on the DISNEY DREAMS CRUISE!

Giving something, even a little bit, will create a priceless experience and lifelong memory for our dear friend Jen and Corbin. Our goal is to raise $5000 to send them on this one of a kind, simply amazing cruise....it's the very LEAST we can all do.

We love you, Jen!!!
Jill, Mollie, Lindsay, Emily, Jessi and Robin

The goal…$5000 in six weeks? Incredibly admirable! What was even more amazing was they raised the money in 48 hours and they had to shut the fundraiser down after a week because they didn't want to risk me being taxed on the money if it went over ten thousand. There was enough money to completely pay for not only the cruise, but our airfare, shore excursions, and truly priceless memories!

I worked with a travel agent to quickly plan the trip around my chemotherapy schedule. We were able to stay in an upgraded room on the cruise ship complete with a private balcony. We were on the ship with the famous, state of the art Aqua Duck water coaster that goes over the edge of the ship! It wasn't completely perfect; Corbin got sick four times the first night. I almost lost it—I was at sea, didn't know anyone, had a sick child, and didn't think I could survive four more days of this. I thought it was supposed to be vacation! Thankfully he rebounded and found his sea legs on the second day.

Corbin and I were able to participate in a shore excursion at the utterly stunning Atlantis resort. At Atlantis, we were able to swim, jump, and climb on their water playground. We laughed as we rode inner tubes down the lazy rapid river and cheered as we went down the water slide. After seeing my pictures and videos from Hawaii, Corbin asked if he could come with me next time I swam with dolphins. We were able to participate in the dolphin encounter at Atlantis. We were able to hug, pet, and even kiss a dolphin! We took time to tour the incredible aquarium at Atlantis. We also went to Disney's private island, Castaway Cay, and Corbin went in the ocean for the first time. We watched fireworks on the boat while at sea one night and the next day watched the movie *Cars* on the outdoor big screen while swimming.

While I don't know who gave what amount, I can tell you that 75% of the donors were friends from the Greek system at SIU. Considering that in the Greek system there is such a small portion of the student population, it is evident what strong bonds were created. At a time when the economy is in despair, people gave generously to send Corbin and me on a Disney cruise…how amazing! Dreams really do come true!

These truly priceless memories were made possible by the group of friends I met sixteen years ago! They've been a huge part of my life for half of my life. They are generous with their friendship, everlastingly loyal, and incredibly giving in their love. My quality of life would be severely diminished without them. Thank you to each of you; I love you!!!

March 2011, L-R:
Jessi, Emily
Lindsay, Robin, Jill, Mollie, me

May 2011: Corbin and me on the Disney Dream!

Magic 4: Wonderstruck

You saw me start to believe for the first time...
You are the best thing that's ever been mine
Taylor Swift, "Mine"

I knew of Taylor Swift and her music, but she wasn't really on my radar. I wasn't the president of her fan club, I wasn't first in line to buy her album, nor could I sing along to all of her songs. Then, she released a single called "Mine" in the summer of 2010, and I really connected to that song because of the relationship I was in.

A few months later that summer, I was at the mega store picking up groceries, when I saw her newly released CD called *Speak Now* and bought it on a whim. I went home, played it, and was smitten with the lyrics. When the song "Last Kiss" played, I started bawling. The song spoke to my very broken heart—as the first man I cared for post-divorce had just ended our relationship. What's remarkable about the song is that anyone can relate. None of us know when we're going to have our last kiss, hug, and/or conversation with someone we love.

After listening to the entire CD, I thought, "I feel like a twenty-one year-old superstar has been spying on my life and has written an album about it!" There were songs about love, revenge, broken hearts, friendship, and the support of loved ones. I know I'm too old to be a groupie, but I admire

Taylor Swift. She's elegant, classy, and insanely talented. She plays multiple instruments and wrote all of the songs on her latest album. Oh, and let's not forget she's the perfect height! I decided that one of the Magic 7 had to be: attend a Taylor Swift concert. I never really thought I would meet Taylor Swift, but I now know that God will surprise you when you least expect it.

Many people have asked; how the heck did you get to meet Taylor Swift?! My answer: "It was purely a gift from God." It is almost impossible to get tickets to her shows, let alone get a meet and greet. Only God could pull something like that off!

In December 2010, I was in Chicago with my best friend, Ashley, to see *Wicked*. We drove up the evening before the show and went to dinner at Webber's Grill. We started talking about making a "bucket list," which eventually became this; The Magic 7 of 2011. I listed:

See Taylor Swift in concert
Attend the Ellen show
Go to Hawaii (or somewhere I've never been)
Swim with the dolphins

Then I said, "Wow, those are all really big, expensive things," so I added: Dance on a bar.

The next day, while still in Chicago, we went to lunch with a good friend. We happened to mention the bucket list conversation from the night before. He knew someone in L.A. who might be able to help us get tickets. Sure enough, that friend came through, and we purchased our tickets in March for the July show in Indy.

A week before the show, we decided to have t-shirts made saying "Survivor loves Swift" with "Bucket List: Meet Taylor" on the back. Our group of four, including my sister, Ashley, and another friend, were hoping to get picked from the 13,000+ in the audience. I posted the shirts on Facebook less than forty-eight hours before the show to flaunt the design as my excitement for the concert peaked!

Several of my friends were trying to pull strings to help me meet Taylor Swift. One member of my church, Dave, emailed that his sister-in-law's brother works on the fourteen buses and twenty-two semis for her show. We left for Indy and hadn't heard anything, but then I got a phone call from Dave stating: "Jimmy (his distant relative) said the office said 'no.'" Dave then said, "Jimmy said, 'I just don't want God to think I didn't try hard enough, so I'm working a different route.'" Dave said he'd call back as soon as he heard anything. When Dave called he said, "I've got some bad news, Jen. There's only one bracelet. YOU'RE GOING TO MEET HER!" We drove like a wild banshee to get to Indy in time. My friends dropped me off at the arena as I anxiously hurried in to will call to pick up my bracelet.

When our group of 75ish people got to go downstairs, we were told absolutely NO photos/videos/cell phones etc. could be present. They would take a picture of us with Taylor and post on the website where we could download a personal copy. The two girls behind me in line had the brilliant idea to turn the video component on, put the camera in our pocket and simply make an audio recording. Here's a transcript of what was said. As the two people in front of me left, one commented about Taylor being tall.

Taylor: People always say that I'm taller or shorter than they expected.

Then I entered, she gave me a huge hug and said, "Hello, how are you?"

Jen: You are the perfect height, just as I expected (she's 5'11", just like me), but I'm in flats and you're in heels.

Taylor: You're beautifully tall.

Jen: So are you; takes one to know one.

Cheese for the picture

Jen: Thank you so much. It's an honor to meet you!

Taylor: How are you doing? Are you doing well? Are you in remission?

Jen: No, no. Should have been dead in December (statistically) but I'm here to see you tonight.

Taylor: Hang around, ok?

Jen: I will; I'll be out there rocking tonight!

Later I was able to call and personally speak with Jimmy and thank him for the amazing amount of work he did to get this to happen. Jimmy was just as gracious (and Southern) as Taylor. It turns out his mom lived for three great years after being diagnosed with breast cancer.

Another sneaky friend was working behind my back to try and get us pit passes so we would be closer to the stage. There is another famous country song about unanswered prayers. This happened to be a great example of that! The crowd was almost all female, and probably more than half were girls under the age of twelve. We were four adult, single women. Right after Taylor made her entrance, one of my friends noticed some guys our age had just come to the seats literally the row behind us. Turns out it was Need To Breathe, the opening band and one of my sister's favorites. We were able to snap a few pictures with them, and my sister, Sara, chatted with them for a while for her own personal "meet and greet."

We were thrilled to tell our families about what an amazing experience we had! A few weeks later, I asked my mom, "What are you doing Sunday afternoon and/or evening?" She said she didn't have anything going on. So I told her I had a surprise for her.

I went to my parents' house that Sunday afternoon and told my mom, "I figured since you come with me to all my not-so-fun appointments in cancerland, I should treat you to something fun. We're going to Taylor Swift's concert in St. Louis tonight—surprise!" The look of pure shock on her face was priceless!

When we got to St. Louis, I noticed the big semis parked outside the arena. I suddenly had the idea to call Jimmy, who got me the meet and greet in Indy. I was able to reach him, much to his surprise! My mom and I were able to meet him, which was such a small way of thanking him for believing in God when I didn't think it was possible. While Jimmy wasn't the perfect height like Taylor, he was humble and polite and introduced us to a few other of the crew during our brief chat. In Indy, I got to meet Taylor. In St. Louis, I got to meet Jimmy, who is a superstar in his own right.

Which Is Bigger: My Smile Or Her Talent?!

Magic 5: Jax

**Children are the living messages
we send to a time we will not see.**
Neil Postman

My father is from Cleveland, Ohio, and my mom is from Columbus, Ohio. They met while in college at The Ohio State University. They married and moved to Columbia, Missouri for my father to work on his master's degree in entomology (the study of bugs—how exciting). My mom was a nurse at the local hospital. They lived in a simple ranch home with an enormous backyard.

My brother, Eric, and I were born in Columbia. I have faint memories of living there—one of my favorites is going to visit horses at the stables at the University of Missouri. I have always had a love of horses and as a child I had plenty of toy model horses. I remember playing with them one day and making one jump over a fence. The ear of the horse was so pointy that it cut my eyebrow. My dad colored the butterfly bandage to look like an actual butterfly, placed it over my cut, and it healed perfectly. I remember telling Eric that we had "magic berries" growing in the backyard. After he ate some of the berries, I got into serious trouble. Eric had to drink syrup of ipecac to induce vomiting since the unknown berries were likely poisonous, not magic. Don't worry, as we grew, he quickly outsmarted me and got me back plenty of times!

Then we moved to Champaign, Illinois when I was five for my father's new job. My sister, Sara, was born there. We lived on a cul-da-sac full of children our age. There was a creek where we caught crawdads. There was a small wooded area where we built forts. There was a pond where we went fishing and even caught a snapping turtle. There was a swing set in almost every back yard. We spent plenty of time playing outside with the dozen children that lived in our neighborhood.

We also spent plenty of time in the car traveling back and forth to Ohio at least twice each year to see our grandparents and extended family. As a child, I thought the six to eight-hour car ride seemed like an eternity. Then again, it was probably worse for my parents hearing "She's looking at me!" or "Are we there yet?" or "I have to go to the bathroom…again."

When I was married, I was thrilled that my immediate family and my spouse's extended family were close to Champaign. When Corbin was born, I was thankful we could celebrate each holiday with both sides of the family. I was so happy that he would see his extended family often due to proximity.

Since Corbin is an only child, I wanted his relationships with his extended family to be close since he doesn't have siblings. Then with the divorce, it was up to Corbin's father to maintain that relationship with his family for Corbin's sake. My brother, sister, and I are very close; we joke that if you combine the three of us together, you'd have the perfect, well-rounded child. I am your stereotypical social butterfly. My brother is the brains of the bunch, going to Michigan

State University on a full academic ride in computer science. My sister is the athlete of the family, playing basketball at Wheaton College, and then helping coach, in addition to a full-time teaching job, after her playing days. When my brother married Christy, she perfectly added to our original trio with her fashion sense and upgraded not only our wardrobes, but our lives.

Growing up, our parents instilled in us core values of integrity, compassion, and having family as the first priority. One of the best pieces of advice I ever received was from my brother. I was in graduate school in Chicago and struggling with a decision. I emailed my brother about it and wrote, "I wish God would just shove me in the right direction." His reply was simple, but profound, "God doesn't shove, he whispers. Are you listening?" Yep, he's definitely the brains of the bunch.

My family has a close bond, and Corbin was beyond spoiled being an only nephew/grandchild. He loves to go visit my dad at his farm and ride on the tractors. He loves snuggling with my mom reading books. He rough-houses and plays endless hours of video games with my brother. He plays tag and pretend with my sister. In essence, he has all the attention he could ask for.

Then came the exciting news that my brother and his wife, Christy, were having a baby! I knew one of the Magic 7 would be becoming an aunt! Since cancer permanently destroyed my fertility, I was thrilled at the opportunity to snuggle, spoil, and love on a new baby! My brother teases me, but one of my favorite smells in life is a newborn. And one of the most precious sounds in life is hearing a baby coo.

Eric and Christy nicknamed the baby "the nugget." Knowing they would need all their vacation time for maternity/paternity leave, they were unable to join the family in Disney World. As we were exiting Corbin's favorite ride, my mom noticed a sign that said "Nugget Way," so we giggled and excitedly talked about the new addition to the family.

Sara and I were in Hawaii when their ultrasound was scheduled. We were in a touristy shop when my phone rang. We put Eric on speaker phone, and he announced, "There's going to be another little Arnold…it's a BOY!" We were jumping up and down screaming, and then we explained the situation to the startled store clerk. We then learned his name would be Jaxson Cade, nicknamed "Jax."

Jax was due in late August; however in the middle of July I received a text from my mom saying, "Christy's water broke. Headed to the hospital. Keep her and Jax in your prayers." Jax was going to be born six weeks early. My brother, Eric, was born a couple weeks early, and when he was born, his lungs weren't completely developed. So Eric was in NICU for several weeks. I remember putting on an adult size gown on my four-year old little body to go visit my very sick little brother. Thankfully Eric grew into a healthy child and adult. But, knowing that past made this present situation even more alarming.

One of my most vivid memories in life was feeling how warm Corbin was when he was laid on my stomach after delivery. I was able to snuggle, kiss, and nurse him. In contrast, after a difficult delivery, Jax was rushed to the NICU. Many hours later, Eric was able to see him, and almost 24 hours later, Christy was finally able to see him. Thankfully, Jaxson's lungs were fine, but he struggled with being able to suck and swallow. Eric and Christy practically lived at the NICU for a week and a half. Then Jaxson was strong enough to come home. And I finally got to hold my nephew!

Although almost 5 years separate Corbin and Jaxson, I know they will be close growing up due to the strong values of family instilled in us by our parents. Right now as an infant, Corbin thinks he's *pretty boring*, but I can't wait for the day when he's teaching Jax all of his tricks! In the meantime, I'm looking forward to experiencing all of Jax's firsts as he grows, and I can't wait to hear him utter "Aunt Jen" or his own special name for me.

With My Favorite Boys, Corbin and Jax

Magic 6: The Best Medicine

For me, it's that I contributed, ... That I'm on this planet doing some good and making people happy. That's to me the most important thing, that my hour of television is positive and upbeat and an antidote for all the negative stuff going on in life.
Ellen DeGeneres

Growing up in Illinois with the former queen of daytime talk filming a few hours north in Chicago, I knew many people who went to Oprah's show. Not me…Oprah is too serious. I set my sights on something more in touch with who I am. I wanted to be in the audience of *The Ellen DeGeneres* show, so I could dance and laugh. Laughter is the best medicine, right?

The tickets are free but very hard to get because they are requested so quickly. In August, I was excited to find out that requests for the tickets were available online. I decided to try for the biggest experience possible; I wanted to go to the breast cancer show. I figured if I have to live with this disease, I might as well try to get some free giveaways out of it. I knew the show doesn't air live, so I randomly picked a date a few days before October (Pinktober) hoping it would all fall in place.

I went on with my busy life and honestly forgot about the request when I didn't hear anything in the next few days. I got the phone call about ten days after requesting the tickets.

I was at my parents' house screaming, smiling, jumping up and down; you would have thought I just won the lottery! And in my mind, I did! Laughter and dancing are something money can't buy! During the conversation with the representative from the show, I explained my situation (young, breast cancer) and said I was hoping to attend the filming of the breast cancer show. I was put on hold then told they didn't know that far in advance if/when they'd tape the breast cancer show. I was offered four tickets, which I gladly took. Then I was faced with an incredibly hard decision—whom to invite.

Whenever I mentioned that one of my goals was to see Ellen, almost everyone said, "Oh, I want to go too!" However, when it came down to work schedules, childcare issues, and health issues it was supposed to be my friend Erin from Orlando and my friends Shannon and Brandie who live in the Los Angeles area. They were also young and diagnosed around the same time I was. We all originally met online, but then we had also met at several conferences. The four of us cancer gal pals were going to dance and laugh on Ellen—talk about the best medicine!

The week before the show, Erin found out she had to have emergency surgery to support the vertebrae in her neck where cancer had eaten away the bone. The road to recovery would be long and unfortunately she would not be able to attend *The Ellen DeGeneres Show* as she was just getting out of the hospital. Erin was one of my biggest *Live Legendary* teachers and now she was sidelined due to cancer complications. Erin was bold in the way that she loved life. She was the one who taught me that being a cancer patient is a full-time job. Erin

44

was passionate about travel, had a fierce fashion sense, and was always an absolute blast to be around. I was disappointed that she couldn't make the trip, but heartbroken knowing she was in so much pain requiring surgery.

I had chemotherapy on Monday, flew to L.A. on Tuesday. Shannon, one of my cancer gal pals, picked me up at the airport and after a brief reunion of screams, hugs and tears; she asked what I wanted to do. My reply, "Something touristy and fun!" so we headed to Hollywood Boulevard. We parked and walked around the corner. I noticed a huge crowd in front of the Hard Rock Café. As we walked by, I asked the security guard, "What's going on?" He replied, "Melissa Etheridge is getting her star on the Walk of Fame." Shannon and I looked at each other knowing that Melissa was also a fellow survivor. For a moment, we were able to meet her. She rubbed my fuzzy head and briefly offered her advice and support.

After lunch, we decided to do a tour of Hollywood homes, which became comical because our tour guide was so passionate about his job. Then, we went to Madame Taussaud's wax museum and took hilarious pictures posing with the wax celebrities. Finally, we headed to Brandie's, our other breast cancer gal pal's, house for another mini-reunion and hopefully a good night's sleep.

I felt like a kid on Christmas Eve imagining all the possibilities of the next day! We signed up for a VIP tour of the Warner Brothers lot, then would eat lunch, and head to *The Ellen DeGeneres Show*! I normally sleep ten or more hours, but with all the excitement, I was lucky to get a desperate four hours of sleep.

Even with the lack of sleep, I woke with pure adrenaline pulsing through my body! We each quarantined ourselves to our respective rooms to get ready—otherwise we knew we'd talk and giggle and never leave the house on time. Since Erin was unable to make the trip, one of Brandie's neighbors was able to use her ticket.

We went on the VIP tour which was fun, but there were no celeb sightings. Next we ate lunch, and then headed to the waiting area for Ellen. While in the waiting area, we were instructed to fill out surveys with our basic information and questions for celebrities scheduled for the next day's show. Then we learned that Heidi Klum, LeAnn Rimes, and Nancy Pelosi would all be on the show that day!

We walked from the waiting area through security, which rivaled TSA, then to the riffraff room for more waiting. Brandie had a connection to get us bumped up to VIP seating which meant we were towards the front of the line to file in and sit in the actual studio. They told us which four chairs to sit in, which happened to be on the aisle and in the row Ellen dances across. I couldn't have picked better seats myself!

While I was busy filling out my survey, Brandie and Shannon were sneaky and wrote a brief note on the back of their papers. Before taping starts, the warm-up comedian comes out and gets the crowd going. The energy and excitement in the studio is palpable! Everyone is up and dancing, smiling, and having a great time. Once when the warm-up comedian passed by us, Shannon gave him the notes they wrote. He shoved it in his back pocket. I said, "He probably thinks you just gave him your number!" laughing because he had a wedding ring on.

Up next, the grand entrance! All the sudden we heard Ellen being introduced and watch as she walks out from behind sliding doors. Ellen completes her opening monologue, the crowd is laughing, and then we all start dancing. I catch her eye and smile as she dances up the stairs right past me! She completes her dance through the audience and takes a seat for the first commercial break.

During that commercial break, one of the producers approached me. My first thought was, "Maybe I get to be on one of her games?!" Then I realized she must have received the notes Shannon and Brandie wrote. I briefly explained my situation and why this was such an epic moment to be at the show. She looked at me kindly and said, "I can't promise anything, but we'll see…"

The show continued on; it was a surreal experience. Then while I'm dancing during the second commercial break, I notice that the senior producer is on the stage with Ellen and they're looking in my general direction. I wasn't sure what to do. Wave? Blow a kiss? Act like I don't notice what's going on? Before I can figure out what to do, Ellen is on her feet, climbing the stairs and embracing me in the biggest hug I've had in my life. I clearly remember two things. First, she had *REALLY* cold hands. Second, I thought, "Oh, so this is what a really expensive suit feels like." The show thoughtfully taped the interaction and gave me a copy before we left. From that video I was able to read my own lips; I kept saying, "Thank you, thank you, thank you," as we hugged. Then I pulled out some really awkward dance moves and we posed for a picture.

Shannon, Brandie, and I were all in tears. When Ellen pulled away from the hug, she had tears brimming in her striking blue eyes. She is incredibly gorgeous! She went back to her chair to finish the interviews and show. After the show she thanked the audience for coming, and said, "I know for some of you it was harder to get here than others. What's your name again?" pointing at me. "Jennifer," I replied. "Jennifer, sending you all my love." Then she exited the stage.

I lost count of how many times we said, "Did that really just happen?!" that evening. We exited the studio, purchased a few things for ourselves and some things for a care package for Erin. As we walked back out on the street we saw a huge black SUV. The windows were all tinted, but the back window was down. I looked, it was Heidi Klum! So I yelled, "Heidi!" She turned, looked, smiled, and waved to our group of four. It was the perfect ending to the perfect day.

I left beautiful, sunny, warm LA and returned to the flat cornfields of Illinois the next day. Although I was in LA for 48 hours, it was some of the most incredible memories of my life!

This chapter is in memory of Erin Painter Howarth,
April 13, 1977 – October 17, 2011

Shannon, me, and Brandie

Ellen and me

Magic 7: Searching for Mr. Perfect

Listen to your heart.
Even though it's on the left side, it's always right.
Unknown

After going through a painful divorce in 2009, I decided to give the New Year a theme. I went with "2010: The Year of Jen." It was my time to heal. To learn to love and be loved. To explore who I am on my own without a significant other. I had been a serial monogamist. I had the same boyfriend throughout college. The next person I dated, I ended up marrying. I didn't know what being single felt like nor did I have a clue about the "rules" of dating as an adult. Looking back, I'm thankful for that time. I grew so much. It was a struggle and at one point it was excruciating, but ultimately it was for the best.

One of the most important lessons I learned that year was that I am loveable. I'm sure anyone who has gone through a divorce questions their own lovability. Being young and a single mom often equates to "baggage" in the dating world. Add multiple scars, treatment induced menopause, and Stage IV cancer, and I thought I was damaged goods: a lost cause. Don't get me wrong; I have the most incredible support system! My family is insanely hilarious, forever encouraging, beyond thoughtful, and incredibly loving. My friends are fiercely loyal, focused, completely precious and great in number. I had everything I needed - except romantic love.

I didn't think someone could love me for who I was at that exact moment in time. I thought potential partners would see me as someone broken with an uncertain future. I know I sure did at times! Then I met, became friends with, and fell deeply in love with a man. He taught me to laugh uncontrollably, to trust without reservation, and most importantly: he taught me I am loveable. He also taught me that love comes in all forms. I joked that compared to my *usual* type, he was too short (easily an inch shorter than me), too old (fourteen years older than me), and too uneducated (although highly accomplished in his profession he didn't earn a college degree). He also shattered my delicate heart when he walked away from the relationship unexpectedly. I was in disbelief over his decision; I thought true love conquered all! Only now, more than a year later, I can understand he needed to learn to love himself again—much like I needed to learn to love myself after my divorce. Although this relationship was so much shorter, the break up was insanely more painful than the divorce.

In the time since the break up, I've learned to let my heart heal. I've given myself permission to grieve a love where I felt so fulfilled. And, in total honesty, I've put the guard back around my heart in hopes of never experiencing that pain again. I've let myself become comfortable with me at the purest form again. And, I've finally set my sights on the real Mr. Perfect!

There is a term that anyone in cancerland loves to hear, "No Evidence of Disease" or as I affectionately call it, NED. NED is my Mr. Perfect! This is as close to a "cure" as is actually possible once someone is diagnosed with cancer.

After a diagnosis at any stage, there will always been some sort of follow up test or scan for the rest of your life. Hearing that there is no evidence of cancer in your body is like finding the Holy Grail. For some people, it comes easily…others, like me; continually try to obtain the status of NED. We stalk him feverishly yet never quite find him.

The next best thing to Mr. Perfect (NED) is his best friend, Stable Mable. This is when a scan shows that although there is still cancer in the body, there is no progression. The current treatment, whether it is chemotherapy, radiation, anti-hormonal treatment, or targeted therapy is working and holding the disease steady. Of course the hope is always that the cancer melts away and NED is at my doorstep. But, if that love affair is in the distance, I'll hang with my BFF Stable Mable for as long as she'll have me.

And I did have a brief encounter with Stable Mable, which made The Magic 7 of 2011 complete! I am incredibly thankful that I was able to complete each and every one of the Magic 7 of 2011, and none of them would have been possible without *YOU*. This book is my small way to try and give an enormous "thank you" to *you*. Without you, my list would be unfulfilled. But, more importantly, so would my life. Thank *YOU* for being one of the biggest reasons my *Quality of Life* is excellent - even if my Quantity of Life is uncertain. I love you.

Xoxo
Jen

Jen's Top Ten

There are many opportunities to support cancer-related organizations and charities. These are my top ten favorite cancer-related charities that don't have million dollar marketing budgets, so you may not have heard of them. Big corporations have already established their place in *Cancerland*; however, they often have little direct impact on a personal level. I can assure you that these charities are making a difference in the lives of individuals. Next time, when thinking of making a donation, please consider these charities.

Breast Cancer Action
http://www.bcaction.org
Advocate for more effective and less toxic breast cancer treatments by shifting the balance of power in the Food and Drug Administration's drug approval process away from the pharmaceutical industry and toward the public interest. Decrease involuntary environmental exposures that put people at risk for breast cancer. Create awareness that it is not just genes, but social injustices — political, economic, and racial inequities — that lead to disparities in breast cancer outcomes.

Breast Cancer Recovery
http://www.bcrecovery.org
All retreats are designed by breast cancer survivors for breast cancer survivors. Breast Cancer Recovery embraces all women with breast cancer including all faiths, ages, races, sexual orientations and financial resources. Women in all stages are welcome to attend - from the newly diagnosed to women many years in remission. Women ages 20 - 71 have attended a retreat. Solo retreat and Mets retreat available.

Conference For Young Women

http://www.c4yw.org

Each year, at this gathering, you'll get the chance to:
Hear updates from leading professionals who have dedicated their lives to caring for young women with breast cancer
Learn about new scientific research and clinical care breakthroughs set to offer meaningful benefits to young women with breast cancer or those at risk of developing it
Network with other survivors—share stories, get advice and experience the joy of meeting someone who understands

I'm Too Young For This!

http://www.stupidcancer.org

The I'm Too Young For This! Cancer Foundation is a non-profit organization that empowers young adults affected by cancer through innovative and award-winning programs and services. We are the nation's largest support community for this underserved population and serve as a bullhorn for the young adult cancer movement. Our charter is to ensure that no one goes unaware of the age-appropriate resources they are entitled to so they can get busy living.

Imerman Angels

http://www.imermanangels.org

Imerman Angels provides personalized connections that enable 1-on-1 support among cancer fighters, survivors and caregivers.

Memories of Love

http://www.memoriesoflove.org

We help create lasting and loving memories by sending the entire family for five days to Orlando, Florida for a fun-filled vacation far removed from mounting medical bills, therapy and hospital visits. Through the generosity of corporate partners and sponsors, we are able to provide tickets to the area's best loved theme parks: Universal Studios / Island of Adventures and SeaWorld, as well as a beautiful room at one of a number of Orlando/Kissimmee Resorts, discount meal vouchers, and financial support for travel and incidentals.

Metastatic Breast Cancer Network
http://www.mbcn.org
MBCN is a national, independent, nonprofit, patient advocacy group dedicated to the unique concerns of the women and men living with metastatic breast cancer . We strive to help those living with stage IV breast cancer be their own best advocate through providing education and information on treatments and coping with the disease.

Metavivor
http://wwww.metavivor.org
We are a 501(c)(3) non-profit organization run entirely by volunteers, mostly with MBC. We created METAvivor because we believe the following: Support for MBC patients is greatly lacking; Awareness of the disease is appalling low; BC mets research is horrendously under-funded.

Pink Daisy Project
http://www.pinkdaisyproject.org
The Pink Daisy Project is a 501(c)3 organization dedicated to helping young women with breast cancer manage treatment a little easier. PDP provides gift cards for groceries, gas, or housecleaning to help young women undergoing treatment.

Young Survival Coalition
http://youngsurvival.org
Young Survival Coalition (YSC) is the premier global organization dedicated to the critical issues unique to young women who are diagnosed with breast cancer. YSC offers resources, connections and outreach so women feel supported, empowered and hopeful.

Acknowledgements

The original intent of this book was to acknowledge the many people who made The Magic 7 of 2011 possible. In addition to those people, my humblest thanks go to Teri Fuller and Joanna Strauss. I'm so grateful to Teri's dedication to helping extract the stories and edit the book. I appreciate Joanna's willingness to work with me to design the book cover.